SEO

20 Search Engine Optimization
Tricks to Get Your Website to
the Top of Search Results

By ERIK FISHNER

Table of Contents

Introduction

Search engine optimization involves writing, designing, and coding of a website in a way to improve the quality and volume of traffic to your website. The marketing strategies are selected on the basis of the target audience and the nature of the business. SEO is one of different marketing practices and it should be a part of an overall advertising strategy. Your marketing plan may include both offline and online advertising techniques. There are numerous SEO techniques that help you increase potential customers on our website. The websites with a large number of visitors can get higher rankings and get top place in the rankings of search engines.

SEO is frequently growing facade of web design and advertising. You can build your website in a framework that makes it easy for search engines to understand. Some people are unable to understand the importance of SEO, but it is really significant to increase the ranking. For a web designer, the Google is not a search engine, but it is a system for reputation management. The majority of people expect to get top ranking for their brands at the top results of search engines. With the help of SEO, you can increase the visibility of your products. You will need simple search terms called "Keywords" to increase the visibility. The traffic will come through this keyword.

SEO can deeply observe each and every aspect of your website because a web design is not for looks and feels. It should smoothly work and your website should have the ability to convert as per different devices. It is important to implement SEO and there are two ways to implement, such as content and coding. Content means text and the information to share with customers. This is the most important part of SEO because search engines attempt to find the most relevant search results for users. You have to focus on landing pages, headings, titles, keywords and flow of the website pages to engage users.

There are numerous components of SEO that will help you to increase the rankings of your web pages. This book is designed for your help so that you can learn 20 search engine optimization tricks to get your website to the top of search results.

Chapter 1: What is SEO and why it is important?

Search engine optimization aka SEO is really important for your website. SEO is a set of rules followed by a blog or website to increase the search engine ranking of their website. This method is really useful to increase the quality of your website to make it easy and fast to navigate. The SEO can be taken as a framework because the whole procedure has a few particular rules and stages. SEO depends on numerous factors, such as the on-page structure of HTML, the architecture of the website, website content, inbound links, use of keywords and collective content on a domain.

Why is Search Engine Optimization significant?

In today's competitive era, SEO has great significance than ever. The search engines serve millions of people on a regular basis who look for the answers to their questions or solution of their problems. SEO can help you to grow a blog, website or e-Commerce stores. The SEO is important because:

- Good practices of SEO can improve the experience of visitors and usability of a website. The users trust search engines to get their required material and the search of users can increase the trust of a website.

- SEO is good for the social promotion of your website. People often find your website in Yahoo and Google searching and they use social media websites to promote your work. It can increase productive traffic on your website.

- The SEO is significant for the smooth running of a website, online web store and other eCommerce sites. They can directly increase the traffic and indirectly benefit the framework of your website.

- It can help you to compete with your competitors because by increasing visitors, you can get the advantage of more sales and maximum customers.

Main Stages of SEO Procedure

SEO can't be known as a static procedure, but it is a framework with rules. There are two main stages of SEO, such as:

- On-site SEO: These are rules applied to your website to make it friendly for search engines

- Off-site SEO: It means the methods used for the promotion of your website or blog that can help you to get better ranks in search results.

Difference Between SEO and Internet Marketing

SEO is an important tool, but some people mix it with internet marketing campaigns. In fact, SEO and internet marketing are different tools. Internet marketing can be a part of SEO because the websites are often promoted on social media pages. Both methods are like oranges and apples. These two platforms work together to increase the growth of online business.

The main purpose of the SEO is to bring the website of your company to the front page and the first link in the search engines. The page rank is based on the SEO; therefore, the companies focus on the relevant content and keyword density.

Internet marketing plays an important role in the success of the business because it basically focuses on the interaction between people through video marketing, article marketing, and social media. The social media play an important role in the promotion of content. Online forums are really important to use in the internet marketing.

An important SEO factor is Social Signal, and it puts the consumer in charge of Page Rank. Every time, the users "Tweets" or "Follow" a blog or article and it affects the page ranking. The backlinking is an old method, but it is still beneficial to build a strong reputation of an original website. Good quality content along with frequent blogging can affect the Page Rank.

The internet marketing strategy requires good quality content to promote the brand. It enables you to send sales copies through email to existing and new customers. The call-to-action helps people to read the website and buy anything offered by the company for sale. The online campaign and the business should put its major focus on SEO and half focus on the internet marketing.

Chapter 2: 20 Search Engine Optimization Tricks for Top Ranking of Your Website

SEO is a hot topic on the web because everyone wants to get a higher rank and get more traffic. There are 20 useful tricks that can help you to get your website appeared on the first page:

Trick 01: Title Page

Before starting anything, it is important for you to select a title for your business because it can be the hardest part. This small piece can be a marketing puzzle for you because this can be the biggest factor in the success of your business. Your Meta Title will be based on the actual title. The Meta Title plays an important role in the SEO ranking.

Meta Title

The Meta Title and Meta Descriptions are hidden elements on your page that are important to portray your site on Google, Yahoo and other search engines. These elements give a unique taste to your website and people come across to your website with the use of small words. Google will recognize your company with the help of details given in the Meta Title about your products and services.

Tips to Write Meta Title

The basic structure of meta title for a local organization is:

Keywords | Name of Your Business | Location of Organization

If you are running an online business, you can omit location. The Google gives you a limit of 70 characters to write the Meta title, but it will be good to keep it between 50 and 55 characters, counting spaces.

Always remember that the title will not look similar to each search result. When someone writes similar words for a search query, the Google will make the matching words of your title bold.

You can use vertical bars to keep the things separate on your site to make it easy for search engines to read your title.

The Meta Title may also appear on the tabs of browsers and social media pages. You should consider the clarity and quality while writing a Meta Title.

The title of your business should be catchy enough to match with the search results of the users. When the words of meta title match up in the search query, the Google will bold the matching words and place your website higher. In order to get positive results, you should make efforts to find out the words used by users. The "Google Adwords Planner" can be a good choice to fine-tune the title of your business.

Trick 02: MetaData Description

Meta descriptions are HTML attributes to offer a concise explanation for the content on your web pages. These are basically used on the result pages of search engine. MetaData plays an important role in the search results because it helps you to describe the content of your web page.

Tips to Write Meta Description

Use action-oriented language because it is excellent for call-to-action and it helps readers to get an idea about the content. It will be good to start with action verbs, such as "Grab, Get, Discover, Learn and Follow", etc.

Use a short sentence to explain about the nature of content to the reader and offer them clear benefits of clicking a particular link and reading your post. You can sell them in a better way with the help of valuable and informative content.

The meta description should be less than 155 characters including spaces. Google actually measures pixels instead of characters. It will cut your description after a particular width; therefore, 155 characters are taken as a benchmark.

It is not good to deceive searchers because if the description deceives searchers, they will immediately leave your website. It is not good to use keywords in the description because it will be considered as spamming and hurt the level of trust of searchers in your content.

The meta description should be specific and relevant without fluffy words. You should do your best to grab the attention of the audience and help them to understand the content of your article.

Trick 03: Creation of Content

Content is really important for the promotion of your website and there are some tips regarding the creation of useful content:

- You should perform an audit to determine the existing content of your company to find out what is missing and what more can you have. It will be good to make a portfolio of your products and understand the needs of customers.

- The content should be strongly relevant to your products and needs of your customers. Add urgency to your content, such as availability for a limited time or limited stock. For instance, if you want to share an eBook, you can make its first 50 pages free for people who register their account to your website. It will force customers to buy your eBook to read remaining pages. Give something special to your customers on initial purchase so that they can get the advantage of your products.

- While creating content, you should consider your audience to increase their appeal in your content. It will be good to focus on the events, seasons, holidays and other events to increase the chances of engagement. It will increase trust between you and customers along with chances of sales.

- You will select a topic for your content, select a user-friendly language, explain its effects on the reader, explain your recommendations, discuss issues and give a call-to-action at the end.

- If you want to write interesting content, you should put yourself in the shoe of the reader. Try to find out their issues, describe the outcomes of these issues and offer solutions. You can use anecdotes, metaphors along with analogies to create effective content.

- Your content should be free from any distraction, such as directly publish content on landing pages. Avoid excessive links, distracting images and irrelevant items on the landing pages. It will be good to add another voice to your websites, such as a testimonial, interview and other things to show that your services are authentic.

- It is important to give a call-to-action, but it is not good to give only a pitch to your content. You should give advice to your customers and then write a "Get it, buy it, read it" and other similar phrases.

Trick 04: Google+ Profile

Google+ is an excellent way to build an energetic community because it is a social network of Google. You can make new contacts and curate circles on the basis of your interested, design, news, business, etc. Google+ can be an excellent platform to promote your products and services. There are some tips that will help you to create a powerful Google+ account:

- You should select a neutral name for your account that looks professional and it should be similar to all social media accounts. For instance, S. Taemin on G+, Twitter, and other social media accounts. After making an account, modify your URL, such as https://plus.google.com/+STaminr/posts, instead of, https://plus.google.com/+5477778/posts.
- In your profile, you should write about yourself and your activities. It is important to explain that how your activities can be helpful for followers. Make your profile unique by writing your passion, hobbies, interests, social channels, blogs, etc. Your profile should look professional and for this purpose, you should select a professional picture to display on the profile.
- Your account should have a memorable tagline so that people can remember you for a long period of time. You

should make a meta description containing 160 characters. You need to completely fill your profile information to provide all maximum details to your followers.

- You need a unique cover page and the size of the photo should be 1080 x 608. You should display your particular brand on the cover page so use a professional logo and communicate the passion in your life. You will stay consistent with your cover page to make it your brand.

- Keep your followers engaged by sharing your expertise, thoughts, vision, emotions and values. You can share shot out your website and blogs along with quotes and inspirational thoughts. Follow people in your industry and create a conversation session.

- It will be good to view your Google+ profile as others may view it in an "incognito window". This type of window can be found in the file menu of Chrome.

Trick 05: Make sure to Get Your Site Indexed Quickly

If you want to index your site quickly, there are some instructions that will help you with every new domain:

In the first step, you should determine either your site in indexed in any search engine. For this purpose, you can check your website by opening Google and then type site:name.com (you should replace the name with the actual domain name, such as "fashioncity.com") and check whether the site is indexed. In case of no results, you have to follow given below steps and get into the Google:

Indexing refers to search engines maintain records of your web pages. The search engine bot comes to your site and it starts crawling on the basis of your index meta tags or noindex tags. The search engine adds web pages with index tags; therefore, some people often use robots.txt to place the sites in search engines in a few hours. The "robots.txt" is considered a standard use by the web sites for the communication with web crawlers and web robots.

Before you index your new website, make sure to prepare your content because Google bots will crawl your empty home page. You have to do basic SEO, such as titles, meta titles, meta descriptions and then follow the next steps.

Make sure to check the index status of every website and submit every blog in blog directories and networks. You should avoid link directories related to link exchange. You can start with Blogcatalog because it can drive lots of traffic to your website and always links back to your blog.

XML Sitemap Submission

A sitemap is created for the crawlers to productively crawl your blog and a well-created site map can be really helpful.

Now submit your sitemap to Google, Yahoo and Bing along with any other search engines.

The sitemap helps you to organize your website and an XML of Google was designed for search engines to let them find data at a faster rate. You need to learn XML construction to create a sitemap from scratch or you can get the advantage of online tools, such as sitemap generators available for your help. After creating it, you have to submit it to major search engines to index your website thoroughly. It is important to update your sitemap on a regular basis after creating the new content on your website.

Webmaster Tools

Webmaster tools of Google can be good to index your web pages. It also helps you to submit your XML sitemap and provide essential information on the indexing status of your site. You can change the indexing rate of your website and get help thoroughly. It offers you a chance to see crawl errors that

Google has faced while trying to index your pages and check the stats of Google crawling.

Interlink Internal Pages

Keep it in mind that linking and structure of your website can be influenced by the ways your website is indexed by Google. If the spiders of Google enter through the homepage of your website, they will continue the rest of the website through internal links. It is important to work on the internal link structure and your content should be easily found through this link structure. You should solve the internal link issues by creating a sitemap (HTML) of a website that may consist of links to all pages of your website.

Create Fresh Content

Fresh content may attract the spiders of Google because the content is a king. You should create new content or update existing content to attract the crawlers of Google to regularly return to your website.

Links Back Internal Pages

People often focus on the homepage only for link building, but the link building should be a part of your SEO and try to link internal pages as well. It is beneficial for deeper indexing of your website via Bing and Google. Deeper indexing may improve traffic and conversion rate of your website.

Trick 06: Landing Pages

Landing pages are web pages that serve as the entry point for the particular section or the whole website. It is important to optimize your web page to increase the performance of PPC campaigns and ROI. You should create compelling landing pages by taking care of the following components:

- Headline and sub-headline
- Brief description to increase the value of landing pages
- One relevant image
- Security badges and testimonials (optional)
- A form to collect information about visitors

Remove the Basic Navigation

When the visitor arrives on the landing pages, it is your duty to grab their attention and keep them there. You should not use links that can distract visitors and you will not be able to retain them. You should increase the conversion rate of landing pages to reduce the led generation friction. There are lots of marketers, blockers and other factors that can distract or turn off your potential lead.

Match the Heading to the Landing Page

You should focus on the call-to-action (CTA) and the heading of landing pages. If the headline and CTA are different, it can create confusion. In order to reduce all confusion, it is important to consistently reflect your CTA promise on the landing pages.

Less is Better

You should keep everything simple and apply this similar philosophy on all landing pages. The clutter can distract or confuse visitors. You should focus on landing page friction and keep everything simple and to-the-point.

Focus on the Offered Value

You should use a few bullet points to highlight the benefits to highlighting the value of your website. It will increase the productivity of your website and help you to address particular problems.

Social Sharing

It is important to include social media sharing buttons on your social media sites. Make sure to limit clutter and keep everything clean so that someone can use his/her personal account to contact you.

It will be good to create more landing pages and offer maximum, but relevant information to increase the value of your landing pages. You need to add a privacy message and form to get sensitive information of customers with security seals. The form should be short enough to avoid any irritation to customers and they can fill it comfortably.

Trick 07: Snippets

Page titles and descriptions often called snippets and this can be completely automated. The basic goal of the snippets along with the title is to represent each result in a better way. It should relate to the query of customers. It is important to create a descriptive page title to explain what is on the site. There are some quick tips for titles:

- The description should be short and concise.
- Avoid keyword stuffing because it can look your title spammy to search engines.
- Avoid any repetition or boilerplate because long titles are also bad.
- You should brand your homepage and website titles and keep them concise.

- The robots.txt protocol on the side can stop Google from crawling your pages.

Trick 08: Inbound Linking Tactic

There are some link-building tactics that can help you to boost your off-page SEO:

- You have to submit your website to directories to have complete control of the website. The inbound link may not give full authority, but it is an important part of link-building efforts.
- You should create remarkable content (link bait) to grab the attention of others and encourage them to link your website. If your content creates value for the target audience, others can automatically try to link it to their videos, original data and other conversation topics.
- It may take more time in networking and relationship building, but it is really effective for your business. You should consider the interest of people while creating content and start building relations with relevant websites and authoritative bloggers. You can follow them on Twitter and optimize your social media presence.

- Some websites may use "no follow tags" and you will not be able to get SEO juice from links on the social media profiles. You should carefully use social media profiles and point them to direct the viewers of the website.

- The new release is a great way to share words about the news of your products and other important updates. Guest blogging and leveraging partnership can also help you to generate inbound links.

Trick 09: Outbound Linking Tactic

The backlinks provide a way to assess the authority of the website other than the on-page text. Backlinks were taken as an outbound link on the website and these were counted as the vote in the favor of your favorite destination site. The outbound links are really important because the outbound link structure can prove helpful for the visitors. With the help of outbound links, you can increase the creativity of your website for customers.

You can incorporate outbound links to provide more information on a complicated topic. You can link to the niche sub-topics, such as if you are selling ice cream, you can link ice cream machines on your website. The outbound link encourages you to keep links in the body of the article as useful anchor text. Make sure to select informative text and avoid any spam activity.

Trick 10: Rank for Quality

You can get the advantage of quality to increase the rank of your website. The quality score may vary by Yahoo, Bing, and Google. It can influence the rank of your page and cost per click. There are some factors that play an important rate to determine the quality score:

- Click through rate
- Ad copies relevance
- Landing page quality
- Landing page load time
- Geographical considerations

You should avoid any spamming and use unique and quality content to get the advantage of quality.

Trick 11: Ranking in Google Image Search

A picture worth 1,000 words and a unique image can benefit your business after getting ranked in the image search. The image can generate TON of traffic to your website. There are some quick tips for image optimization:

You can use Alt Text because this text can help the search engine to understand images. It is easy to add alt= "write your alt text" to tag your image.

"<img src="girl-smiling.jpg" alt="Girl Smiling" />"

You should consider the size of your file because a large file can increase the page load time. Be careful while adding an image because the browser may resize the image. You have to stop this process by inputting height and width tags. You can use an image editing program to resize the image as per your desires.

Name of your file is another important factor to consider

Before uploading the image, you should consider the file name that you want to use for the ranking of the image. It will be good to do a simple search for their file name.

You should give a caption to your image after considering the bounce rate. The image caption is the most well-read pieces of the image. It can decrease your bounce rate and increase the ranking of your website.

Trick 12: Perfect Press Release

Press release is an essential part of the good public relations. This compelling document shares details of products with customers and there are some tips that will help you to design an effective press release:

- Start with a compelling title that should reveal the half story to customers about your announcements. A strong headline should be engaging and attractive.
- The first paragraph will contain the important point to engage readers. You should address the significant points in a few lines. Subsequent paragraphs will support this information.
- You should include hard numbers, such as quantify your claims and argument to make it more compelling for readers.
- It should be free from grammatical errors and you can include quotes whenever possible. You should include your contact information and provide access to more information by sharing your website.

Trick 13: Blog for SEO

A blog post can play an important role to rank your website because you can share keyword-rich topics on your website to increase the online visibility of your web store. It will be good to use Adwords tools to generate keyword ideas and get better ranking. There are some tips to increase the visibility of your website:

- You should start with a few keywords because the search engines give more importance to the keywords.
- You should deal with number list to engage your customers, such as 10 tips to improve your love life, 3 questions to ask in an interview, etc.

Colon can help you because a couple of keyword phrases look appropriate with a colon. For instance, it will be good to write "Fast food Recipes" instead of writing Asian Culinary Blog. In the last step, you can finalize your writing by checking in the SEO plug-in.

Trick 14: Elevate Your Trust Factor

The trust factor is a combination of numerous factors and a trustful site will get a higher rank on Google searches. There are some factors that can affect the trust of your website, such as low-quality content on your website.

- Privacy policy, disclosure, and terms are some factors that are really important. This can be a good sign that your website is legitimate. The information on the contact us page and the information given at the time of registration should be same.
- The length of the content is another factor because the longer article, unique content and regular updates can increase the trustworthy status of your website.
- Is there any trusted source on the website? A trusted source will help you to get good rankings on the search results of Google. While sharing a link, make sure to avoid the similar niche in which you are working. You should not help your biggest competitors.
- Video content can increase the ranking of your website and for your website, you can select YouTube videos for more views and high ranking.
- High-quality links are also important to build a trustful image of your website. It is not easy to get high-quality

links; therefore, you can create good quality content and share with others.

Trick 15: SEO Tools

There are numerous SEO tools that can help you to increase the ranking of your web page and make your work easy. There are numerous tools, such as Page Rank Checker, SEO Toolbar, Meta Tag Generator, Keyword Suggestion tools, keyword list cleaner, keyword list generator, hub finder, local rank, SEO site planner and lots of other tools that can prove helpful for your website health.

Trick 16: Rank of Author

Google can perk up the quality of search by linking it to the author's digital signature. The authorship will help you to link your articles on Google+ profile. The Google+ circles can increase the strength of online presence and social media activity will also help you. The quantity and quality of comments can engage your audience. The quality and volume of inbound links are required for the author's content. To get better author's rank, you should create killer content and build an internal as well as external team.

Trick 17: Power of Social Media

- You can triple your revenue with the help of a twitter account.
- The use of Facebook, LinkedIn, and Tumblr pages will help you to build a good reputation.

The social media platform is excellent for you because you can increase the return on investment. You can build a social circle that can help you to increase the profitability and revenue of your business. You should make a social media account and get the advantage of these accounts.

Trick 18: Target Your Interest Graph

Facebook makes a series of changes in the search on the interest graph. You can index search results with the help of hashtags, people, locations, and posts.

Check competitors and analyze the search results on the basis of competitors. You can design content suitable for your needs, search hashtags, and descriptions to give an edge to your writing.

Trick 19: Keyword Density

Keyword density is a percentage of repetition for a particular word or phrase to appear on the web page. The keyword should be used appropriately because the optimum density is 1 to 3 percent. The overuse of any keyword is called "keyword stuffing." Keyword stuffing can be the reason to penalize your web page. There are some online tools to calculate keyword density, but you can also use the following formulae to calculate density:

$$Density = (Nkr / Tkn) * 100$$

$$(Nkr * Nwp/Tkn)* 100$$

- Nkr means how many times a specific keyword will be repeated
- Tkn means total words in your article
- Nwp means the number of words in a phrase.

Trick 20: URL Structure and No Follow Link

You should keep the structure of your URL simple so that the people can easily follow them. You should not use unreadable words and long ID numbers because these are not good for the health of your website.

No Follow Link

No follow offers a way for the webmasters to give a message to search engines to "don't follow this link on the page". The Google will not transfer the PageRank or anchor text of these links. The use of "no follow" will help you to drop the target link to your graph of the web. You can use no follow links to avoid spamming content.

Conclusion

Search engine optimization aka SEO is really important for your website. SEO is a set of rules followed by a blog or website to increase the search engine ranking of their website. This method is really useful to increase the quality of your website to make it easy and fast to navigate. The SEO can be taken as a framework because the whole procedure has a few particular rules and stages. SEO depends on numerous factors, such as the on-page structure of HTML, the architecture of the website, website content, inbound links, use of keywords and collective content on a domain.

SEO is a major driver of customer acquirement and expansion for eCommerce stores. An effective SEO should include the right keywords on a web page and compelling content to increase the traffic on your website. There is a misunderstanding that effective SEO involves the right keywords on a web page. The SEO touches every part of a website from designing to content. This practice is important for everyone running an online business.